YOUR KNOWLEDGE HAS VALUE

- We will publish your bachelor's and master's thesis, essays and papers

- Your own eBook and book - sold worldwide in all relevant shops

- Earn money with each sale

Upload your text at www.GRIN.com and publish for free

Bibliographic information published by the German National Library:

The German National Library lists this publication in the National Bibliography; detailed bibliographic data are available on the Internet at http://dnb.dnb.de .

Imprint:

Copyright © 2016 GRIN Verlag, Open Publishing GmbH
Print and binding: Books on Demand GmbH, Norderstedt Germany
ISBN: 9783668213906

This book at GRIN:

http://www.grin.com/en/e-book/321285/issues-and-debates-on-diagnostics-and-medication-of-posttraumatic-stress

Raja Sree R Subramaniam

Issues and Debates on Diagnostics and Medication of Posttraumatic Stress Disorder

GRIN Publishing

GRIN - Your knowledge has value

Since its foundation in 1998, GRIN has specialized in publishing academic texts by students, college teachers and other academics as e-book and printed book. The website www.grin.com is an ideal platform for presenting term papers, final papers, scientific essays, dissertations and specialist books.

Visit us on the internet:

http://www.grin.com/

http://www.facebook.com/grincom

http://www.twitter.com/grin_com

Table of Contents

Introduction...2

History 2

Diagnostic Criteria...3

The biological hypotheses of PTSD 4

Animal model of PTSD 5

Gender Differences...6

Age...6

Cognitive Reserve...7

Genetic Factors...7

Sleep...7

PTSD treatment..8

Pharmacology...8

Psychosocial therapies...9

Conclusion..11

References..12

Issues and Debates on Diagnostics and Medication of Posttraumatic Stress Disorder (PTSD)

Introduction

Whether it is war-traumatized soldiers, refugees, victims of sexual assault or victims of catastrophic life events, the psychiatric consequence of the posttraumatic stress leading to a mental disorder if left untreated can be debilitating. The prevalence of posttraumatic stress disorder (PTSD) in countries that have suffered war and political conflicts such as Northern Ireland (Muldoon et.al.2007, p.146), Uganda (Mugisha et.al, 2015,p.2) and Palestine (Canetti et.al.2010, p.219) ranged between twenty to seventy percent. Analysis of epidemiological surveys by the World Mental Health, between 2012 until 2015 for non-war related traumatic event reported 54% of lifetime prevalence in Europe, 56.1% in Italy and 60.6% in Northern Ireland (Atwoli et al., 2015, p.302). Given the potential economic and psychosocial impact of PTSD, efforts to identify biomarkers of risk, disease and treatment of PTSD is of significant public health importance (McCrone et al., 2003,p.519). The psychiatric codification of PTSD has made possible for patients to access medical care and treatment. Likewise, mental health professionals were able to predict reliably, distinguish and diagnose trauma-associated disorder from other major mental illness (APA, 2013). However, the issue of whether PTSD owes its existence to environmental context, individual differences and learning or whether it is entirely neurobiological determined has been debated fiercely (Charney et. al., 2002, p.32). Findings from the neuroimaging and translational research provide evidence that supports the neurobiological theories of etiology but yet to find a specific biomarker for PTSD (Zoladz & Diamond, 2013,p. 890). In fact, research outcome strongly suggest PTSD is a result of interaction between biological, individual predisposition and environmental context.

History

According to Birmes and colleagues (2003,p.18) history of trauma symptoms experienced by people existed in different names long before the formal diagnostic classification status as PTSD in DSM-III in 1980 (APA, 1980). During the 19th century, soldiers returning from the American Civil war were believed to develop traumatic neurotic caused by adverse emotional volatility, nostalgia and homesickness (Birmes et al., 2003, p 18). Analysis of historical war medical files between 1916 until 1918 revealed two hundred cases known as disordered action of the heart and two hundred cases of shell shock disorder, which clinicians during that time believed those conditions rose due to tight chest constricting combat gears, adjustment problems and irrational expectations of war (Jones et al., 2003, p 159). However, it was the impact of Vietnam War on mental health long after the war ended highlighted the need for formal categorization of PTSD. The first health survey on combat fatigue by the National Vietnam Veterans Readjustment Survey revealed that the risk of developing PTSD among the Vietnam War veterans was as high as 30.9% (Kulka et al., 1990a). The findings helped recognize PTSD as a distinct psychological disorder that develop after a traumatic experience such as war. Analysis of Pension file records from the First, Second, Malaya, Korean and the Persian Gulf War revealed clusters of symptoms similar to PTSD, persistent avoidance, hyperarousal and mood alterations with diagnostic labels, for example, shell shock disorder, psychoneurosis, battle hysteria and cardiac neurosis (Jones et al., 2003, p159).

Diagnostic Criteria

Other than combat experiences, evidence of PTSD symptoms among civilian population led to the recognition that PTSD symptoms could be reliably diagnosed and received the formal classification as a psychobiological mental disorder in the American Psychiatric Association's Diagnostic and Statistical Manual of Mental Disorders in 1980 [DSM-III], (NIH, 2010, p1). The International Classification of Diseases, Tenth Revision (ICD-10) by the World Health Organizations (WHO) is another classification system recognizes PTSD as a diagnosable mental disorder since its inception in 1992. Both classification systems of PTSD share similar diagnostic features and also, the current DSM-5 (APA, 2013) has been revised to be compatible with the ICD-10 (WHO, 1992).

According to Jewell and colleagues (2009, p.37) the diagnostic systems adopted a universally understood medical language to facilitate reliable clinical practice among the health professionals without them getting mired in hypothetical disputes about the etiology of the mental disorder. However, critiques argued that the biological model of PTSD has remained descriptive in nature and have not been reliable in actual clinical application (Charney, et al., 2002, p 33). Others concerned that the 'medical' model approach assumes neurobiological basis rather than looking at how environmental and psychosocial factors influence the onset of PTSD symptoms (Suvak & Barrett, 2011, p6). Contractor and colleagues (2014, p146) argued that most PTSD symptom dimensions co-morbid with other major psychiatric disorder, which consequently increases the risk of co-morbid diagnosis. The experts in the mental health field are also concerned the classification spectrums of 'abnormal' experiences risk labeling typical stress responses as a mental disorder (Brewin et al., 2009,p364). According to Charney and colleagues (2002, p. 33) for classification to be valid, the diagnostic criteria should meaningfully classify findings from real underlying etiological assumptions rather than based on clusters of symptoms, which could consequently inform an appropriate treatment and accurate prognosis. These arguments as will be explored impelled researchers to venture into new directions using testable conceptual models to develop valid and functional diagnostic criteria.

The biological hypotheses of PTSD

The biological theory proposes the etiology of PTSD is linked to maladaptive stress responses and neurobiological processes that influence susceptibility and resilience to PTSD symptoms (Depperman et al., p168). According to Koenen and colleagues (2008, p.53), stress responses inherently activate hypothalamic-pituitary-adrenal (HPA) axis by releasing the corticotrophin-releasing hormone from the hypothalamus and adrenocorticotropic hormone from the pituitary and glucocorticoids from the adrenal cortex. The HPA pathway and the sympathetic nervous system together they bind to two types of receptors, the mineral corticoid and glucocorticoid receptors that mediate the fear conditioning in the amygdala, memory consolidation in the hippocampus and fear extinction in the prefrontal cortex (Depperman et. al., 2014, p 170). Persistent pathological conditions of PTSD occur when the limbic structures fail to restore its homeostasis

4

functioning even after 'flight or fight' state no longer exist suggesting the brain's inability to extinguish the conditioned fear response (Jones & Moller, 2011, p.394).

Animal model of PTSD

Fortunately, the development of animal models of predator exposure, Pavlovian fear conditioning, and extinction have allowed translational findings of brain regions responsible for PTSD symptoms, fear circuit functions, the neural plasticity of fear memory and fear extinguishing processes (Daskalakis, Yehuda & Diamond, 2013, p.2) Laboratory simulated stressors such as predator threat; psychosocial behavior and psychogenic probes are used to examine the effects of trauma. Cellular and molecular functions in laboratory simulated freezing and avoidance behaviors observed in the animal models are consistent with neural circuits underlying fear processing in human, with correlational evidence of HPA axis dysregulation, prefrontal cortex, amygdala and hippocampus functioning (Daskalakis, Yehuda & Diamond, 2013, p.3).

However, PTSD research using animal models do not capture all of the PTSD causal attributes and critics argue they are too simplified to account human pathology. For instance, patients receive a diagnosis of PTSD based on their verbal recount of experiences, cognition and understanding skill compared with behavioral assessment of animal models of PTSD. According to Cohen and Richter-Levin (2009, p. 30) differences in stress level and the type of stress between laboratories simulated trauma stimuli such as restraining and foot shock methods may not emulate the same degree or type of traumatic events experienced by traumatized humans. The animal models have a short lifespan and, therefore, evidence of delayed onset of PTSD symptoms that is common in war veterans cannot be studied. Although, the animal models have its limitations, they have provided an abundance of valuable information for the shared benefits of education and potential translational evidence for the development of trials and studies in humans with implications for treatment and therapies (Rasmusson et. al., 1997, p332).

In human participants, functional Magnetic resonance imaging (fMRI) of patients with PTSD has demonstrated similar decreased hippocampal volume as evidenced in the animal model (Bremner et al., 1995, p. 973). Neuroimaging findings suggest trauma-eliciting stimuli activated anterior cingulate, dorsal anterior cingulate, left amygdala and posterior parietal networks that are responsible for generalized hypervigilance (Garfinkel & Liberzon, 2009, p.371). Bremner and colleagues (1999, p.806) reported decreased blood flow in the frontal gyrus in PTSD patients exposed to trauma reminders than healthy controls. Enhanced amygdala activity and decreased prefrontal cortex activity was observed in patients with PTSD than fear exposed healthy participants (Bryant et al., 2007, p. 517).

Although type and severity of trauma exposure are implicated with the risk of PTSD development but the effect of individual differences in stress, coping and adaptation coupled with ecological and environmental characteristics equally contribute to the risk of developing PTSD (Jeremy et. al., 2009,p 44). Jeremy and colleagues (2009) suggested those factors might hold significant indicators to why and what causes some people to be resilient to and others susceptible to developing PTSD symptoms.

Gender Differences

Evidence from animal model and fMRI studies of human brain suggest men and women react to stress and emotion differently. Goldstein and colleagues (2010, p.435) found significant physiological differences in the stress response circuitry, especially the amygdala, hypothalamus, hippocampus, brainstem, orbitofrontal cortex and the cingulate gyrus (Goldstein et al., 2010). The researchers concluded that females have greater fear processing capacity due to naturally endowed high estrogen state than men (Goldstein et al., 2010, p 435).

Age

The formation, consolidation, and retrieval of emotional memories vary developmentally. Kim and Richardson (2010, p 177) revealed very young rats learned to extinguish fear without the activation of the NMDA receptors, but the adult rats took more fear extinction trials for the NMDA receptors to deactivate (Kim & Richardson, 2010, p.177). Thus, the researchers concluded that fear extinguishing training at an early age significantly erases fear associations in the amygdala. The research identified a critical marker for fear resilience with potential development of effective treatment.

Cognitive Reserve

Deary and Batty (2007, p.379) found children who had an intelligence quotient (IQ) >115 during developmental years are more resilient to PTSD in adulthood and suggested the role of cognitive ability in the risk of PTSD. In another study, Hoffman and Mathew (2008,p.249) argued that cognitive reserve play a significant role in extinguishing fear memories and that people who are with lower cognitive reserve may not respond well to cognitive and exposure therapies.

Genetic Factors.

Twin studies comparing monozygotic and dizygotic twins raised in a shared environment showed that PTSD may be heritable, but possible co-morbid with another mental disorder has not been ruled out (Afifi et. al.,2010, p.101). Krishnan and colleagues (2007, p 396) showed molecular adaptations underlying the resilience and vulnerability to a stress-induced environment. The study found differential gene expression, whereby, susceptible mice demonstrated sucrose preference, BDNF signaling, increased anxiety, weight-loss, a sensitized corticosterone and exaggerated response compared with unsusceptible mice. The researchers then compared the findings with human brain specimen and identified an epigenetic adaptation signature in the brain region within the mesolimbic dopamine circuit associated with susceptibility and resistance to symptoms of avoidance in PTSD.

Sleep

Sleep deprivation has been implicated in mediating memory consolidation and restoration of physiological functions (Mohammed et al., 2011, p.39). Mohammed and colleagues (2011, p39) demonstrated neurochemical and electrophysiological changes induced by REM-sleep deprivations affect brain functionality in rats. Numerous findings reveal that sleep; especially the rapid-eye-movement (REM) sleep type facilitates extinction of conditioned fear following exposure therapy (Mohammed et al., 2011, p 41).

Biological, social learning, individual differences and environmental context have been suggested to contribute to the development of PTSD. But, because human brain, mind, and body are interrelated, it is challenging to single out which particular factor influences the development of PTSD. Hence, validating the severity of the illness based on one characteristic of the disorder does not provide sufficient information for clinical decisions. Instead, integrated approach provides multiple scales of diagnostic dimensions that are essential for early detection and treatment intervention in patients with PTSD (Jakovljevic et al., 2012, p253).

PTSD treatment

Pharmacology

The FDA approved drugs for treating PTSD are selective serotonin reuptake inhibitors (SSRi) Sertraline and Paroxetine (Alexander, 2012,p.33). The Clinical Guidelines from the Department of Veterans Affair and the Department of Defense (VA/DoD, 2010), American Psychiatric Association (APA, 2013) and the British Psychopharmacology Society also recommends serotonin-norepinephrine reuptake inhibitor (SNRI) venlafaxine for the treatment of PTSD.

Neuroendocrine systems such as serotonin and glucocorticoid are suggested to generate protective actions in alleviating PTSD symptoms. According to Rasmussen and colleagues (2015, p 2), aberrant activation of various neuroendocrine systems such as serotonin type 2A(5HT2A), glucocorticoid, and yohimbine- induced noradrenergic alpha-2 receptor antagonist increases the risk for PTSD and depression. The SSRi and SNRI drugs are known to replace the serotonin receptor function (Alexander, 2012, p.33). Tucker and colleagues (2001,p.865) found SSRi achieved treatment response rate of 60% with a remission rate of only 20-30% than placebo. The SNRI drug had a response rate of 70% but did not show treatment improvement in patients with PTSD (Alexander, 2012,p.33).

8

Stein and colleagues (2013) argued most of the pharmacology efficacy outcomes are from combat-related PTSD and studies on civilian population provide varying level of treatment outcome. Inconsistent efficacy evidence and severe side effects make the pharmacology treatment of PTSD less preferred treatment option than psychotherapy. Hence, pharmacotherapy is only a second line treatment after psychotherapy because there is no PTSD-specific drugs have been developed (Alexander, 2012, p33). The psychotropic medications are developed to treat symptoms related to other major mental illness. Therefore, treatment is efficacious only in treating symptoms such as insomnia, depression and anxiety (Alexander, 2012, p.33). Friedman and colleagues (2011,p.752) argued problems in randomized research trials; double-blind procedures and small sample size may have compromised the internal research validity affecting the research outcome such that the full potential of drugs in the treatment of PTSD symptoms remained undetected.

Psychosocial therapies

Cognitive behavioral therapy (CBT) for treating PTSD is the first line of treatment (Bisson & Andrew, 2007). The American Psychiatric Associations (APA, 2013), the National Institute for Health and Clinical Excellence (NICE), The World Health Organizations (WHO) and the British Association for Behavioral and Cognitive Psychotherapies (BABCP) just a few examples of organization recommends CBT for treating the PTSD.

Elher and Clark (2000) developed the trauma focused CBT model for PTSD that draws on the CBT models of Beck and colleague's (2009) cognitive and behavior treatment protocol. CBT formulations are developed to help resolve negative thought processes in a collaborative way to identify problematic thoughts, emotions and actions, and breaking them into smaller achievable goals (Ehlers et al., 2005). Besides the cognitive restructuring, the model also includes techniques such as imaginable prolonged exposure, in-vivo therapy, controlled breathing, stress inoculation training (SIT) and eye movement desensitizing and reprocessing (EMDR) whose efficacies have been validated using randomized controlled trials (Bisson & Andrew, 2007, p.187). Two randomized control studies have evaluated the effectiveness of Ehler and Clark's model (Ehlers et al., 2003; 2005). According to the Cochran database of systematic (Bisson & Andrew, 2007, p.187) review CBT overall produces greater treatment improvement compared to patients on the waitlist or treatment as usual.

Trauma-focused CBT (TF-CBT) has been reported to be efficacious in treating PTSD in children, adolescents (Dorsey, Briggs & Woods, p.255) and rape victims (Resick et al., 2002, p.867). Cohen and colleagues (2004, p.395) applied a multi-site randomized control trial and evaluated 229 children aged between 8-14years who have been sexually abused, with 90% of them experiencing DSM-IV PTSD symptoms. The results revealed that children who received TF-CBT scored greater improvement on various PTSD symptom related questionnaire over a course of three weeks compared with children who received child-centered ther-apy (CCT). The TF-CBT model is also flexible in engaging various community and cultural settings and have recorded successful treatment outcome across Asia and Europe (Amaya-Jackson et al., 2003,p.205).

Prolonged exposure therapy (PE) developed by Foa and colleagues (2005,p.953) is useful in teaching patients to examine erroneous thought processes, meanings and beliefs attached to trauma reminding memories and how they distress them. Like prolonged exposure, the in vivo therapy works by gradually exposing pa-tients to trauma suggesting situations, which they have been avoiding (Foa et al., 2005). PE therapy combined with psycho-education and controlled breathing techniques are found effective in treating both chronic and acute PTSD (Foa et al., 2005, p.953). Numerous randomized control studies indicate PE outperforms supportive counseling, relaxation and treatment as usual (Powers et. al., 2010, p.635). Bradley and colleagues (2005, p.216)'s meta-analysis have indicated that PE is as useful as short-term treatment of SSRIs. Comparative efficacies of PTSD treatment studies have demonstrated that PE produced a significantly greater reduction in avoidance and re-experiencing symptoms than relaxation training or EMDR (Bisson & Andrew, 2007, p.205). PE also demonstrated speedier recov-ery rate from avoidance and a proportion number of participants reported to no longer meeting the PTSD criteria after treatment (Bisson & Andrew, 2007, p.205).

Eye Movement Desensitization and Reprocessing (EMDR) is a manually guided therapy for processing information related to disturbing trauma memories, thoughts, believes, emotions and bodily sensations (Power et al., 2002, p297). Numerous randomized control studies suggest that EMDR is as efficacious as CBT treatment for alleviating PTSD symptoms (Bisson & Andrew, 2007, p.213). However, Taylor and colleague (2003,p.331) found EMDR was not efficacious compared to exposure therapies and relaxation training. Meta-analysis of thirty-four studies in various population suggested that EMDR is only effective when compared with non-exposure based treatment but non-efficacious when compared with exposure therapies (Davidson & Parker, 2001,p.305). On the other hand, a systematic review of ninety randomized studies concluded that EMDR has potential benefit in treating PTSD but its efficacy is indistinguishable due to confounding effects of exposure therapy and other factors (IOM. 2008).

Conclusion

Some would claim that PTSD diagnosis does not meet the criteria as a valid psychiatric disorder and that the classification is the result of the influence of insurance corporations and pharmacological manufactures (Biehn et al., 2013, p.291). A counter argument is that the pharmacological and the psychotherapies have helped many individuals in alleviating and in the management of the PTSD. The PTSD diagnostic tools have fulfilled its usefulness in various cultural settings across the world (de Jong et al., 2001). The classification system has led to the development of many effective therapies, treatments and research methods. Perhaps, due to the brain-mind complexity, the PTSD codification could adopt a psychological construction approach to interpreting the biological influence of brain-derived factors, especially where the biological basis of PTSD is inconclusive (Suvak & Berrett, 2011, p. 18). But of course, problems associated with the diagnostic classification systems will be debated and revised, but the core assumptions of PTSD have withstood the test of time (Friedman et al., 2011,p752). In fact, expert analysis, professional opinions, and new research perspectives have led to modifications and revisions that continue to strengthen the validity and clinical usefulness of the PTSD concept.

References

Afifi, T, O., Asmundson, G, J., Taylor, S., Jang, K, L(2010). The role of genes and environment on trauma exposure and posttraumatic stress disorder symptoms : a review of twin studies. *Clinical Psychology Review*. 30, 101-112.

Alexander, W (2012). Pharmacotherapy for Post-traumatic Sress Disorder In Combat Veterans. Focus on Antidepressants and Atypical Antipsychotic Agents. *Pharmacy and Theurapeutics*. 37(1), 32-38.

Amaya-Jackson, L., Reynolds, V., Murray, M., McCarthy. G., Nelson, A., Cherney, M (2003) Cognitive behavioral treatment for pediatric posttraumatic stress disorder: Protocol and application in school and community settings. *Cognitive and Behavioral Practice*.10, 204–213.

American Psychiatric Association [APA] (1980). *DSM-III : Diagnostic and statistical manual of mental disorders. 3rd ed*. Washington DC . Retrieved on 1st October, 2015 from http://www.ptsd.va.gov/professional/research-bio/research/vietnam-vets-study.asp

American Psychiatric Association [APA](2013). *DSM-V : Diagnostic and statistical manual of mental disorders , fifth edition*, Washington DC. Retrieved on 1st October, 2015 from http://www.ptsd.va.gov/professional/research-bio/research/vietnam-vets-study.asp

American Psychiatric Association (APA, 2013), *Treatment of patients with acute stress syndrome and posttraumatic stress disorder*. Retrieved on 10th October, 2015 from http://www.ptsd.va.gov/professional/research-bio/research/vietnam-vets-study.asp

Atwoli, L ., Steinb, D, J., Koenenc , K, C., & Katie, A & McLaughlind, A (2015) Epidemiology of posttraumatic stress disorder: prevalence, correlates and consequences. *Current Opinions in Psychiatry*, 28, 3017-311.

Beck, J, G., Coffey, S,F., Foy,D,W.,Keane, T,M & Blanchard, E, B (2009). Group cognitive behaviour therapy for chronic posttraumatic stress disorder : An initial randomized pilot study. *Behavior Therapy*, 401(1), 82-92.

Besimon, M., Solomon, Z & Horesh, D (2013). The utility of Criteriorn A under chronic national terror. *Israeli Journal of Psychiatry and Related Sciences*, 50, 81-83.

Biehn, T, L.,Elhai, J, D., Seligman, L.D., Tamburrino, M., Armour, C & Forbers, D (2013). Underlying dimensions of DSM-5 posttraumatic stress disorder and major depressive disorder symptoms. *Psychological Injury and Law*, 6, 290-298.

Birmes, P., Hatton, L., Brunet, A & Schmitt, L (2003). Early historical literature for post-traumatic symptomatology. *Stress and Health*, 19(1), 17-26.

Bisson, J & Andrew, M (2007). Psychological treatment of post-traumatic stress disorder(PTSD). *Cochrane Database of Systematic Reviews*, 3, 1-248. Retrieved on 11th October, 2015 from http://www.interscience.wiley.com/cochrane/clsysrev/articles/CD00338 8/frame.html

Bradley, R., Greene, J., Russ, E.,Dutra, L & Westen, D (2005). A multidimensional meta-analysis of psychotherapy for PTSD. *American Journal of Psychiatry* 162(2), 214-227.

Bremner, J., Randall, R., Scott, T., Bronen, R., Seibyl, J., Southwick, S., Delaney, R., McCarthy, G., Charney, D., Innis, R. (1995). MRI-based measurement of hippocampal volume in patients with combat-related posttraumatic stress disorder. *American Journal of Psychiatry*, 152:973-981.

Bremner, J, D.,Staib, L,H.,Kaloupek, D., Southwick, S, M., Soufer R.,& Charney, D,S (1999). Neural correlates of exposure to traumatic pictures and sound in Vietnam combat veterans with and without posttraumatic stress disorder : A positron emission tomography study. *Biological Psychiatry*, 45(7), 806-816.

Brewin, C, R., Lanius, R, A., Novac, A., Schnyder, U & Galea, S(2009). Reformulating PTSD for DSM-V: Life after Criterion A. *Journal of Traumatic Stress,* 22, 366-373.

Bryant, R, A., Kemp, A, H., Felmingham, K,L., Liddell, B., Olivieri, G., Peduto, A., Gordon, E & Williams, L, M (2007). Enhanced amygdala and medial prefrontal activation during nonconscious processing of fear in posttraumatic stress disorder: An fMRI study. *Human Brain Mapping* 29(5), 517-523.

Canetti, D., Galea, S., Hall, B, J., Johnson, R,J., Palmieri, P, A., & Hobfoll, S,E (2010). Exposure to prolonged socio-political conflict and the risk of PTSD and depression among Palestinians. *Transcult Psychiatry.* 73(3), 219–31.

Charney, D, S., Barlow, D,H., Botteron, K., Jonathan, D,C., Goldman, D., Gur, R, E., Lin, K,M., Lopez, J, F., Meador-Woodruff, J, H., Moldin, S, O., Nestler E,J., Watson, S, J & Zalcman, S, J (2002). A Research Agenda for DSM-V. American Psychiatric Association (APA) Washington, D.C. Retrieved on 10the   Octher,   2015   from http://psychrights.org/Research/Digest/CriticalThinkRxCites/CharneyIn Kupfer.pdf

Cohen, J, A., Deblinger, E., Mannarino, A,P., Steer, R (2004). A multisite randomized trial for sexually abused children with symptoms of posttraumatic stress disorder. *Journal of the American Academy of Child & Adolescent Psychiatry.* 43.393-402.

Cohen, H., Richter-Levin, G (2009). *Toward animal models of post-traumatic stress disorder. In Post-traumatic stress disorder* : Basic science and clinical practice. NY. Humana Press.

Contractor, A,A., Durham, T, A., Brennan, J,A., Armour, C., Wutrick, H, R., Frueh, B, C & Elhai, J, D (2014). DSM-5 PTSD's symptom dimensions and relations with major depression's symptom dimensions in a primary care sample. *Psychiatry Research,* 215, 146-153.

Daskalakis, N.P., Yehuda, R., & Diamond, D,M (2011). Animal models in translational studies of PTSD . *Psychoneuroendocrinology*. 1-17 , Retrieved on 1st October, 2015 from http:..dx.doi.org/10.1016/j.psyneuen.3013.06.006

Davidson,P, R & Parker, K, C, H (2001). Eye movement desensitization and reprocessing (EMDR) : A meta-analysis. *Journal of Consulting and Clinical Psychology*, 69(2), 305-316.

Deary, I, J., & Batty, G, D(2007). Cognitive epidemiology. *Journal of Epidemiology and Community Health.* 61(5), 378-384.

De Jong, J, T, V., Komproe, I, H., Van Ommeren, M., El Masri, M., Araya, M., Khaled, N ., van der Put, W., & Somasundram, D (2001). Lifetime events and posttraumatic stress disorder in 4 postconflict settings. *Journal of the American Medical Association,* 286, 555-562.

Depperman, S., Storchak, H., Fallgatter, A, J., & Ehlis, A, S(2014). Stress-induced neuroplasticity : Maladaptation to adverse life events in patientes with PTSD – a critical overview. *Neuroscience*, 283, 166-177.

Dorsey, S., Briggs, E, C& Woods, B,A (2011). Cognitive Behavioural Treatment for Posttraumatic Stress Disorder in Children and Adolescents. *Child and Adolescent Psychiatric Clinics of North America.* 20(2),255-269.

Ehlers, A & Clark,D,M (2000). A cognitive model of posttraumatic stress disorder. *Behaviour Research & Therapy*, 38(4), 319-345.

Ehlers, A., Clark, D, M., Hackmann, A., McManus, F., Fennell, M (2005). Cognitive therapy for post-traumatic stress disorder : Development and evaluation. *Behaviour Research & Therapy*, 43(4), 413-431.

Friedman, M, J., Resick, P, A., Bryant, R, A, & Brewin, C, R (2011). Considering PTSD for DSM-5. *Depress. Anxiety.* 28, 750–769.

Foa, E, B., Hembree, E, A., Cahill, S,P., Rauch, A, M., Riggs, D, S., Feeny, N, C & Yadin, E (2005). Randomized trial of prolonged exposure for posttraumatic stress disorder with and without cognitive restructuring : Outcome at academic and community clinics. *Journal of Consulting and Clinical Psychology*, 73 (5), 953-964.

Garfinkel, S,N & Liberzon, I (2009). Neurobiology of PTSD : A Review of Neuroimaging Findings. *Psychiatric Annals Online* ,39(6), 370-381. Retrieved on 5th October, 2015 from http://www.researchgate.net/publication/240317130_Neurobiology_of_PTSD_A_Review_of_Neuroimaging_Findings

Goldstein, J, M., Jerram, M., Abbs, B.,Whitfield-Gabriell,S & Makris,N (2010). Sex Differences In Stress Response Circuitry Activation Dependent on Female Hormonal Cycle. *The Journal of Neuroscience*. 30(2), 431-438.

Hoffman, E, J.,& Mathew, S, J (2008). Anxiety Disorders : A comprehensive review of pharmacotherapies. *Mount Sinai Journal of Medicines*. 75(3), 248-262.

International statistical classification of Diseases and Related Health Problems, 10th revision [ICD-10] (2008). *Clinical descriptions and diagnostic guidelines.* World Health Organizatons (WHO). Retrieved on the 1st November, 2015 from http://apps.who.int/classifications/icd10/browse/2008/en#/F43.1

Institute of Medicine [IOM] (2011). *Cognitive rehabitation therapy for traumatic brain injury ; Evaluating the evidence.* Washington, DC; The National Academies Press. Retrieved on 15th October, 2015 from http://iom.nationalacademies.org/Reports/2011/Cognitive-Rehabilitation-Therapy-for-Traumatic-Brain-Injury-Evaluating-the-Evidence/Report-Brief.aspx

Jakovljevik, M.,Brajkovic, L., Jaksic, N., Loncar, M., Aukot Margetic, B & Lasic, D (2012). Postraumatic stress disorders (PTSD) from different perspectives : A transdisciplinary intergrative approach. *Psychiatria Danubina.* 24 (3), 246-255,

Jewell, J, D., Hupp, S, D, A & Pomerantz, A, M (2009). Diagnostic Classification Systems . Retrieved on 1st November, 2015 from http://www.researchgate.net/publication/227198943 Diagnostic Classif ication Systems

Jones, E., Vermaas, R, H., McCartney,H.,Beech,C., Palmer,I.,Hyams,K & Wessely, S (2003). Flashbacks and post-traumatic stress disorder : the geneis of a 20th-century diagnosis. *British Journal of Psychiatry*. 182, 158-163.

Jones, T & Moller, M, D (2011). Implications of Hypothalamic-Pituatary-Adrenal Axis Functioning in Posttraumatic Stress Disorder. *Journal of American Psychiatric Nurses Association*. 17(6),393-403.

Kim, J, H.,& Richardson,R (2010). Extinction in preweaning rats does not involve NMDA receptors.*Neurobiology of Learning and Memory*, 94(2), 176-182.

Krishnan, V., Han, M, H., Graham, D, L., Berton, O., Renthal, W., Russo, S, J., LaPlant, Q., Graham, A., Lutter, M., Lagace, D, C., Ghose, S., Reister, R., Tannous, P., Green, T, A., Neve, R, L., Chakravathy, S., Kumar, A., Eisch, A, J., Self, D, W., Lee, F, S., & Taamminga, C, A., Cooper, D, C., Gershenfeld, H, K & Nestler, E, J (2007). Molecular Adaptations Underlying Susceptibility and Resistance to Social Defeat in Brain Reward Regions. *CELL*, 131(2), 391-404.

Kulka, R. A., Schlenger, W. E., Fairbank, J. A., Hough, R. L., Jordan, B. K., Marmar, C. R., et al. (1990a). *The National Vietnam Veterans Readjustment Study: Tables of findings and technical appendices*. New York. Retrieved on 2nd November, 2015 from http://www.ptsd.va.gov/professional/research-bio/research/vietnam-vets-study.asp

Koenen, K.C., Stellman, S, D., Sommer, J, F & Stellman, J, M (2008). Persisting post-traumatic stress disorder symptoms and their relationship to functioning in Vietnam veterans: A 14-year follow-up. *Journal of Traumatic Stress*, 21(1), 49-57.

McCrone, P., Knapp, M., Cawkill, P (2003). Posttraumatic stress disorder (PTSD) in the armed forces: health economic considerations. *Journal of Traumatic Stress*. 2003; 16:519–522.

Mohammed, H, S., Ezz, H, S, A., Khadrawy, Y, A., & Noor, N, A (2011). Neurochemical and electrophysiological changes induced by paradoxical sleep deprivation in rats. *Behavioral Brain Research,* 225(1), 39-46.

Mugisha, J., Herbert , M., Wandiembe, P & Eugene, K (2015)

Prevalence and factors associated with Posttraumatic Stress Disorder seven years after the conflict in three districts in northern Uganda (The Wayo-Nero Study) *BioMed Psychiatry.,* 170, 1-12.

Muldoon, O,T., & Downes, C (2007). Social identification and post-traumatic stress symptoms in post-conflict Northern Ireland. *British Journal of Psychiatry,* 191, 146–9.

National Institutes of Health [NIH] (2010). Fact Sheet-Post Traumatic Stress Disorder (PTSD). Retrieved on 1st November , 2015 from http://www.nimh.nih.gov

Powers, M,B.,Halpern, J, M., Ferenschak, M, P., Gillihan, S, J & Foa, E, B (2010). A meta-analytic review of prolonged exposure for posttraumatic stress disorder. *Clinical Psychology Review,* 30(6), 635-641.

Power, K., McGoldrick, T., Brown, K., Buchanan, R., Sharp, D., Swanson, V & Kaatzias, A (2002). A controlled comparison of eye movement desensitization and reprocessing versus exposure plus cognitive restructuring versus waiting list in the treatment of posttraumatic stress disorder. *Clinical Psychology and Psychotheraphy,* 9(5), 299-318.

Rasmusson, A, M.,Peskind, E, R., Hoff, D, J., Hart, K, L., Holmes, H, A., Warren, D., Shofer, J., O'Connell, J., Taylor, F., Gross, C., Rohde, K., & McFall, M, E (2007). A parallel group placebo controlled study of prazosin for trauma nightmares and sleep disturbance in combat veterans with post-traumatic stress disorder. *Biological Psychiatry,* 61(8). 928-934.

Resick, P, A., Nishith, P., Weaver, T, L., Astin, M, C., Feuer, C, A (2002). A comparison of cognitive-processing therapy with prolonged exposure and a waiting condition for the treatment of chronic posttraumatic stress disorder in female rape victims. *Journal of Consulting and Clinical Psychology*, 70(4), 867-879.

Stein, D, J., Rothbaum, B,O., Baldwin, D, S., Szumski, A.,Pedersen, R., & Davidson, J, R, T(2013). A factor analysis posttraumatic stress disorder symptoms using data pooled from two venlafaxine entended-release clinical trials. *Brain Behaviour.* 3(6), 738-746.

Suvak, M,K., & Barrett, L,F(2011). Considering PTSD from the Perspective of Brain Processes : A Psychological Construction Approach. *Journal of Traumatic Stress,* 24(1), 3-24.

Taylor,S.,Thordarson, D, S.,Maxfield, L., Fedoroff, I, C., Lovell, K & Ogrodniczuk, J (2003). Comparative efficacy, speed and adverse effects of three PTSD treatments : Exposure therapy, EMDR and relaxation training. *Journal of Consulting and Clinical Psychology* , 71(2), 330-338.

The Management of Post-Traumatic Stress Working Group (2010); *VA/DoD Clinical Practice Guideline for the Management of Post-Traumatic Stress: Guideline Summary.* Washington, D, C. Department of Veterans Affairs and Department of Defence, Retrieved on 10th Octoher, 2015, from http://www.healthquality.va.gov/ptsd/mgmt_PTSD_final_92111

Tucker, P., Zaninelli, R., Yehuda, R., Ruggiero, L., Dillingham. & Pitts, C, D (2001). Paroxetine in the treatment of chronic posttraumatic stress disorder: Results of a placebo-controlled, flexible-dosage. *Journal of Clinical Psychiatry.* 62, 860-868.

World Health Organization (1992). *The ICD-10 Classification of Mental and Behavioural Disorders.* Geneva. Switzerland. Retrieved on the 1st November, 2015 from http://www.ptsd.va.gov/professional/assessment/overview/comparison -icd-dsm-iv.asp.

Zoladz, P, R & Diamond, D, M (2013). Current status on behavioral and biological markers of PTSD: A search for clarity in a conflicting literature. *Neuroscience and Biobehavioral Reviews.* 37, 850-895.

19

YOUR KNOWLEDGE HAS VALUE

- We will publish your bachelor's and master's thesis, essays and papers

- Your own eBook and book - sold worldwide in all relevant shops

- Earn money with each sale

Upload your text at www.GRIN.com
and publish for free